Frosted Morning and Midnight

A Collection of Snowflake-Inspired Coloring Designs
on White and Black Backgrounds

By Dawn McAndrew

NOTE FROM THE DESIGNER

I have always been mesmerized by snowflakes and the interesting patterns of frost crystals on windows in the winter, but it wasn't until a few years ago when I came across "*The Art of the Snowflake; A Photographic Album*" by Kenneth Libbrecht that I realized how truly amazing snowflakes actually are. The images of real, natural snowflakes that this scientist captured were astounding and gorgeous- the beautiful symmetry, the nearly-mathematical precision, the unique and never-ending variety...

I had always wanted to create something with a snowflake theme, so, as winter approached this year, I realized that they were the perfect inspiration for my next collection of geometric coloring designs. I very much enjoyed creating this collection and I hope you enjoy adding color to make your own unique creations!

About the Designer/Artist

I am an artist, a writer, an animal-lover, a gamer, and a bit of a geek as well. I have spent most of my adult life working somewhat "traditional" jobs, trying to make ends meet and always feeling as if something was missing. As much as I tried to ignore my need to create and my need to help better the lives of animals, I finally realized that I only felt truly fulfilled when I found a way to integrate them into my life. Now I am focused on my art, writing, gaming, and spending time with my family when I am not working with animals.

"The unruly whorls and eddies in the air drive each snowflake through a chaotic, convoluted path as it grows, resulting in a great diversity of final patterns.

In this way, the wind becomes the artist, creating a multitude of unique ice sculptures using only the simplest of raw materials."

-Kenneth Libbrecht
The Art of the Snowflake
A Photographic Album

TIPS FOR THIS COLLECTION

1) This collection features various individual snowflake shapes which are then duplicated into various patterns and designs. Try coloring an individual snowflake before trying the more complex patterns created with it.

2) There are two versions of each design in this collection, one with a regular white background and one with gray linework on a black background. Consider experimenting with bright or even pastel colors on the gray/black "midnight" versions to create luminous or neon/black-light effects.

3) If you are coloring with markers, place some scrap paper behind the design you are coloring to help prevent color bleed onto the next design.

Happy Coloring!

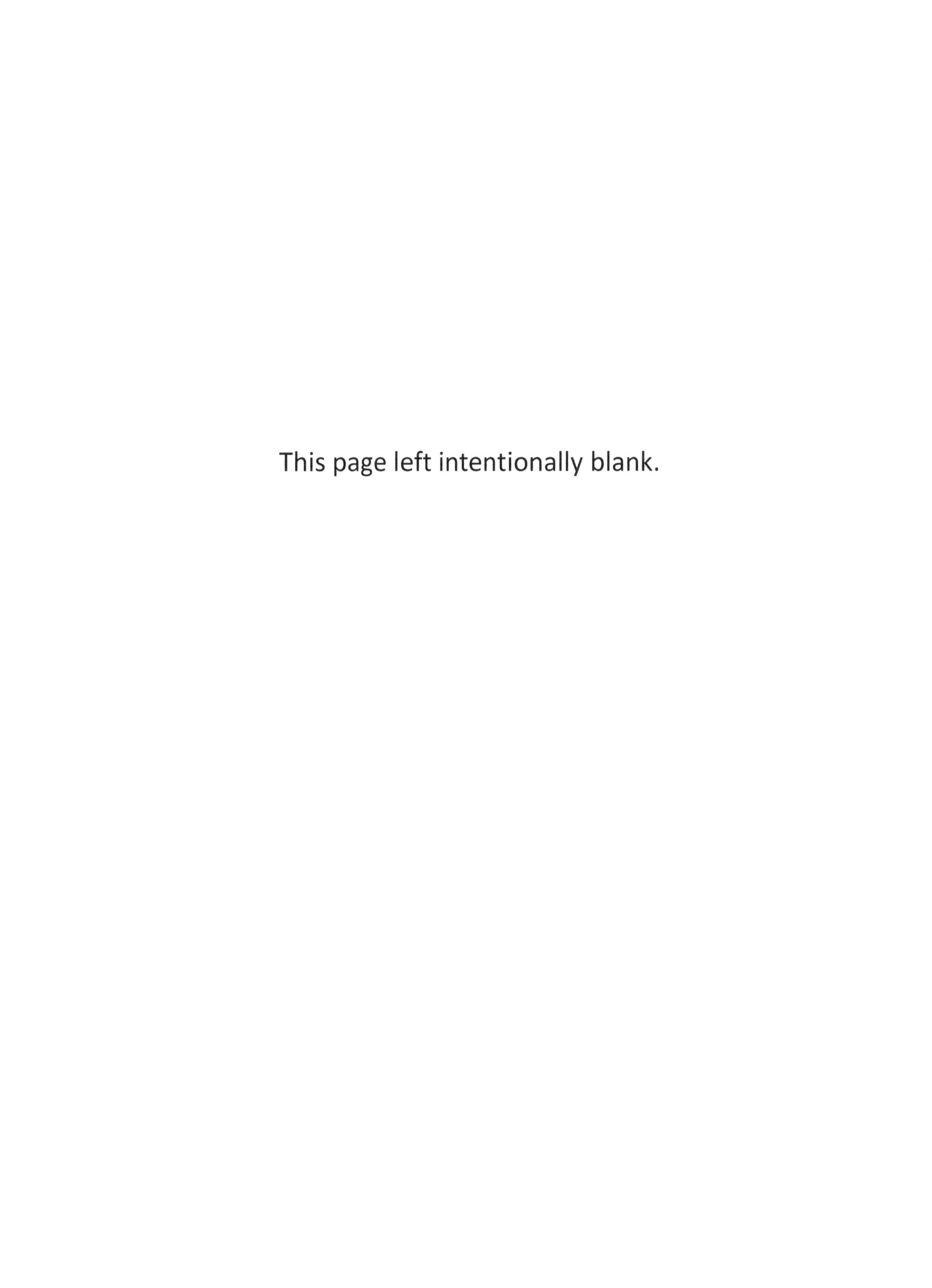

This page left intentionally blank.

--------CUT ALONG THIS LINE--------

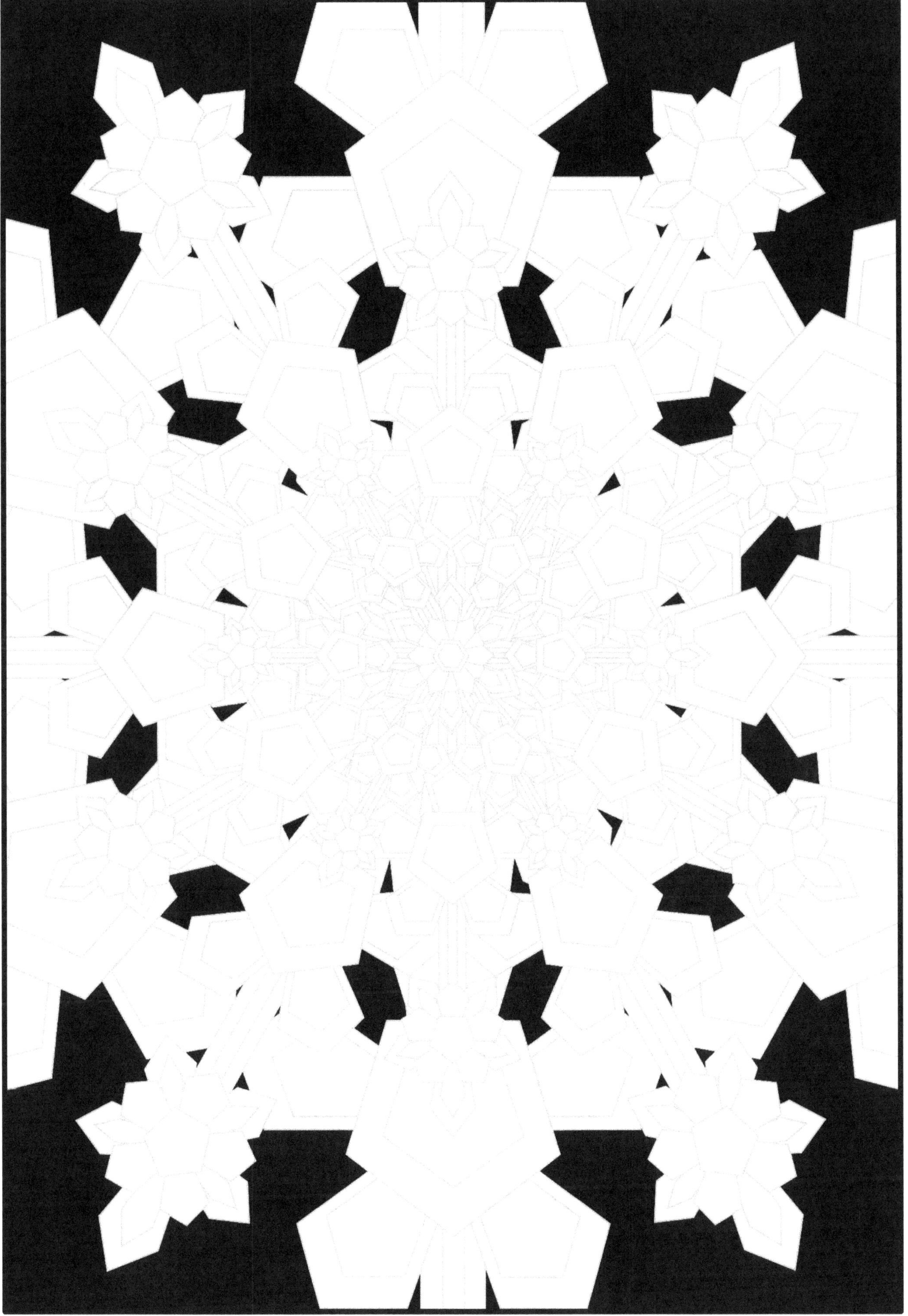

Dear Color Artist,

Thank you so much for giving this collection a chance;
I truly hope you enjoyed completing these works of art!
Please feel free to share your finished versions on
Facebook (https://www.facebook.com/deliriousart.design),
on my website (www.deliriousart.design), or send them via
email to: dawn.mcandrew@deliriousart.design !

This is my second collection of coloring designs and I am
always looking to improve, so I would really appreciate
feedback via my website, email, or on FB. If you purchased
this collection through Amazon, I would also really
appreciate a review- though if there is something negative
please contact me first so that I can try to resolve the
issue!

Sincerely,

Dawn McAndrew

Like the designs in this collection? You may be interested in the following!

Unique Geometric Patterns and Optical Illusions to Color: A Collection of 42 Increasingly Complex Designs For Advanced Color Artists available on Amazon at:

https://www.amazon.com/dp/197610663X

Shop for various tech, home décor, and apparel products printed with these and other designs at:

https://society6.com/dawnsdeliriousdesigns

Downloadable/printable digital copies of various designs at:

https://www.etsy.com/shop/The3DsShopbyDawn